19680   Early Elementary Piano Solo (with optional teacher/parent duet part) $2.50 in USA

Super Kids' Parade

Christine H. Barden

THE ALFRED SIGNATURE SERIES

Super Kids' Parade

Christine H. Barden

Optional Duet Part (Student plays one octave higher)

Super Kids' Parade

Proud march (♩ = 120)

Christine H. Barden

4

Optional Duet Part (Continued)

ISBN 0-7390-2078-1

Alfred Publishing Co., Inc.
P.O. Box 10003 • 16320 Roscoe Blvd. • Van Nuys, CA 91410-0003
www.alfred.com